A florilegium

of Whethers and Wonders

THE WANTON SUBLIME

A Florilegium of Whethers and Wonders

ANNA RABINOWITZ

T|P

Tupelo Press

DORSET, VERMONT

Tupelo Press
PO Box 539, Dorset, Vermont 05251
802.366.8185 • Fax 802.362.1883
editor@tupelopress.org • web www.tupelopress.org

Cover design by Chip Kidd, based on Michelangelo's *Pieta*

Text design by Howard Klein

ACKNOWLEDGMENTS

Heartfelt thanks to the editors of the following anthology and journals for publishing portions of this book:

Barrow Street
Bayou
Boston Review
Colorado Review
Denver Quarterly
New American Writing

"Of Ubiquitous Will" appeared in the anthology, *The Imaginary Poets*, edited by Alan Michael Parker.

Thanks, too, to Timothy Donnelly, Matthea Harvey, Eric Darton, Forrest Gander, Marjorie Perloff, Donald Revell, Bin Ramke, Claudia Rankine, and Susan Wheeler, and especially to Marty for priceless encouragement, support and commentary.

It may be that universal history is the history of the different intonations given a handful of metaphors.

    —Jorge Luis Borges, "The Fearful Sphere of Pascal," *Labyrinths*

also by Anna Rabinowitz

At the Site of Inside Out

Darkling: A Poem

for my children

and to the ineffable magic of being

PRIMARY SOURCES AND FIRST LINES

THE WANTON SUBLIME

OF PLUNDER AND PRECINCT

It begins in a far meadow, a bright room, a hillside thick with time
A woman in a field of flowers interrupted and carried away
A thick of meadow begins it in a woman bright with flowers and time
A room carried in a hillside interrupted a far field away

Had she kept a place in her mind empty to welcome a guest?
And so she played and plucked—lilies from silence
And so she in her mind kept a guest to welcome lilies and
A place empty she had played and plucked silence from

It is a lie that serves the truth
Beauty by nature rules over strength
The truth that serves beauty is a lie
Nature by its strength overrules

A thick silence interrupted in a field of time—a hillside bright with it
Flowers in the mind—in a meadow a room
Is plucked and carried empty to welcome a lie. Her guest
Rules over strength and beauty. And so kept by nature
She had played Woman. It begins far away. She a truth
from a place that serves lilies

Unarmed, unwarned

       must she yield—

                  must she stop—

   a gasp   alas
      aghast   perhaps

        expecting this—

             (whose greeting sneaks
into her peace?)

      at this moment
            sundering syllables right
from his heart

           Hail   thou that art highly favored

        just like that he arrives—

      enters—
         in to her—

            unto her—   in

barges in
      just like that

   comes in and then—

     and now—

           how can she duck

out of this—

        alone—   afraid—

                            poor duck

out of water

        not yet known by man

                  forced here to stop—

(squalls in her breast

                 sudden twitches in

her groin—)

        (Shall she bend to smell the lily—

                   or sneak

another peek at her book—?)

                 IF I AM FAVORED

        LET ME FINISH THIS BOOK—

              (or bolt right

out of this place—

             or look him right

in the eye)

        Listen, you uninvited duck

winging in this way—

             if I am favored

leave me be

    —I've got things to do around the house

            let's put a stop

   to this plot

      Sweat beads in her crotch

               sneaks

down her thighs—

   why me—   *why me*   *what's in*

this for me—

       (elsewhere nails drive in—)

(*coo* to her   *do* to her   do *with* her—)

do *by* her—

right

by her—

do not toy with her—

(must he sneak

in on her between breakfast and lunch—)

poor duck

plucked from—

sucked from—

(what dreams hammer to a stop—?)

it is with great pleasure I tell thee thou art favored

(the looked-up-to turns away—)

favored, favored

for what—

(wanting to flee but leaning in—)

Mary   Mary

not contrary

at Gethsemane your garden stops—

with cocky swells and modest belles—

what a fine crop—

right

green are the grasses of grief—

out in the yard a red-billed duck

takes off for the lake—

as in there was an opening down the road—

a sneak

preview of the way which is not home

                                                          that sneaks
into the scene
              out of the distance—
                                                    terrain favored

with going on—

              because of *must*
                            because of *be*

                                              because nobody ducks
out of this Baby—

                                  Mary it's your chance to step in—

for the good of—
              the need of—
                                  (might even be fun—— **right**—?)

favored
        chosen
                              oh finest fruit at full STOP
in the enactment STOP

              this unraveling STOP

                              as it sneaks STOP in

through your favorite door STOP

              raining harder now STOP   so duck right

down STOP (or out) STOP

              duck if you can STOP   but you can't STOP

              now he's come

                                              STOP

from *A GALLERY OF UPPER CASE SCAFFOLDING*
      AS ANOMALOUS VERSE

obed in R

    wrapped in R

                   rapt by R

         entrapped

         and captive there

Skirting a dappled porch / parch—

      a haunt of languor in a witting / witted set

       a neediness alarmed /

             disarmed
               by angels

   a heart unarmed
          in evernow

     PERHAPS SHE SHOULD NOT HAVE GONE OUT ROBED IN R

(In an initial of easy virtue)

       rod of I   round of O

      (a length of limb limned stepping out)

    letter liquid sensing head   a head rousing

   (the event alights

     where it will go is a tale sealed by its lips)

ram of I   plush of O

(a union there?)

I   and   O

and

I   O

You

R

mine

An apparition in a splash of cloud

(or a real thing)

gilds the room

THE LIGHT CANNOT BE EXPLAINED; IT CAN ONLY BE SEEN

Will you be mine—

(A horizon of gold
splayed down—

illegible

inaudible

(ingots in her head?)

(the horizon knows only desire before it
only desire at its rear

(the horizon is the fierce bleating
of pieces of plot pleading for

place

space   trace

It is the speed of black

        the glut of black
     a day copulating with a maiden's fate

        It is the domination of an endless wound
(no longer will

        she will not / cannot

           will the willing while…

It is the suck sucking

          speed speeding

      increasing

        spinning out of/into itself

it is the gluttony of gravity

    streaming one way

       NO EXIT COMING BACK

     (w)rap of **R**

         tap/

          TRAP OF **R**

(There are ways of recognition
      but his facial features are strange to her)

In her afterthought answers quake

   : one must study an object a long time to know its sign
   : like the intermediate somewhat between a thought and a thing

      and did you

       and will you

   and who is this

Day ~~breaks~~ brakes   light spills

(Wool-scarved villagers idle by

                    prattlers chatter in the hills)

She lifts hands and eyes

     THE LIGHT CANNOT BE EXPLAINED; IT CAN ONLY BE SEEN

Quick

       turn your desire to the *white exploit*

           shepherd of portents
              (mentor of signs)

      may you shimmer
              in the coming gloam

Look
      seek the light, turn your eyes to faithful white

             ever-brightening,
                   obedient,
           dense,
                intense
        WHITE—

            flake white flowers

            purl through sour vinegar,

        cerussa, cerosa, album plumbum,
              albus, glaucus, leucos…

    hues take cues
          to be claimed anew

Look

    somewhere

        someone

      weaves veils of shade

        something unhinges the heartbeat of why

translucent leaves
        breeze the trees

THE VERTIGINOUS THRILL OF EXACTITUDE STEALS AWAY

SPECULUM AND SHADE

A great destiny broods under her skirt

A shapeliness craves yes

                        (O lassitude of folds unfolding)

     And on her yes a future world depends

 (Mystics, husbandmen tend

      wheat fields and grapevines while this is going on)

Do they know

                    all the parts of a good picture
                    are involved with each other
                    not just placed
                    side by side

do they know
           meaning need not be known

    NOR THE LIGHT EXPLAINED

               HER EYES CANNOT DENY
          THE OBLIGATION TO PERCEIVE AN OTHER

      ...JUST SHE AND HE
  EYE AND ITS PASTURE,
        VISION AND ITS VIEW

           AND HER HANDS...

                  trembling to curtail the distance

   where shall they find their peace/place?

from **MIRROR OF THE WORLD**

… whan thou spekyst of any gentilnes, myldeness, or humylyte…
ley thy handes upon thy breste…

And whan thou spekyst of any heuenly or godly thynges to loke vp and pointe towards
the skye with thy finger.

And whan thou spekyst of any holy mater or devocyon to holde up thy handes,

…and whan thou spekyst of a solemne mater to stande vp ryghte with lytell mevynge
of the body, but poyntinge it with the fore fynger.

ON ALL HANDS AT HAND HANDILY

good hands

      time to throw in / up your hands

        all hands on board

your hands

   oh cleanest hands

  give me your hand
      in glove *your hand in the matter*

    do not bite the hand that feeds
    unused-to-this hand

      hold my hand
   touch what is at hand

      (or out of hand
       outhandish one)

   hand it to her

     lend her a hand
      take in hand

        an upper hand
         won if by hand

   oh hand-picked one

      in the palm of his hand

who hands her over

    do not hand her round

must she clasp this hand

     now it's at hand

   HANDS OFF

oh bird in the hand

    wash your hands of this

   lily in hand

at hand

on hand

    hands on

        hands up

           hands out

               hands full

    stay his hand

      play your hand

          hand to hand

Desire installs itself in the eye
                        and embroiders veils

How can this be

In maidhood she abides

                I've not had sex with any man

                I know not a man

        I know not man   **I know no man**

HEAR ME   **I am a virgin**

                as it is said: she has not *known* a man

                        yet her eyes receive an other

        (Desire is specific when desire is real)

WHATSOEVER HE SAITH UNTO YOU...

Frescoed in the field
       crocus, rose, violet, narcissus
            shudder

       (Tipped off?
                Yearning to rest in place?)

Europa,
      she of broad face, water-loving willow,
                 avatar of dew,
          resettles the fuschia folds of her robe, bends low,

           proceeds to

    snip and pluck

A white bull sidles up to her,
      purrs, whines,
          murmurs, hums—
              rubs his nose against her dress,
                  inhales her loveliness

             and the loveliness of her flower cache
               alert to prods of Asia
             and the rushing pulse of lust

    —*Love to love you, baby*—cool he croons—and

    Out comes the gypsy in her

She tits-for-tat the razzle-dazzle guy,
      climbs onto his sparkly back, and grabs a gleaming horn

      certain she's the one who dominates

But, pity, please, the plot's screwed up

The bull's eye's snagged her butt

He gallops, sprints,
breasts the surging sea,

              lifting higher

       the prize he's snared—

And Europa—
          cargo in his hold—

      scared to death

    her tunic now the purple sail
of a great white vessel

                    speeds from her life…

La Morenita   Little Darkling

       coherence of bric and brac, soul and flesh

       have you explored your house, its dark night,
              the forest of your urge?

    face en face

          Lord make your face shine upon her

              Lord make light *shine out of darkness*

heat her heart,
      prowl her groin,
           sail down rivers of her veins

           THE LIGHT NEED NOT BE EXPLAINED

Oh face she cannot see   see *through*

        to where, to whence—

        why me   *why now*   *why here*

"I am that I am"

           He is who He is

      Deal no more with dreaming dreams or dreams of dreams—

The divine descends as weather

a sudden rain flecked with gold

a chill plunged through smoldering, sparking fire

(angry now, she turns away, her thumb saves her place
in the book she longs to finish reading

(her mouth turns down, a frown asserts itself between her brows

(she is taken by surprise at the well
looks up
away

astonished
fearful

(a peasant girl arrested here

(she holds on to a column for dear life

(hostess: *come right in, I'll make a cup of tea*

(a girl with plans: *don't stop me now*
I'll listen but I do not want to hear

(submissive: hands folded across her breast

(troubled
(wary
(cringing at the corner of her cot

(the limits of her sex

The morning is interminable

she wearies of it

the light, how can one face this light

(the slim road dissolves; winds rear up

She is forgetting what she wants to say…

from *A DISQUISITION ON UNBEARABLE CONUNDRUMS OF BEING*

Multiple choice:

1. The morning takes off, clapping its hands: *see you later and take care—*

2. The morning, unwilling witness to this surrender, turns on its heels in disgust.

3. The morning, tickled pink by sunlight and soft breeze, stretches out to bask in the compliance.

4. The morning, having prior knowledge of a fraught night in which an inquisition may have taken place, crawls away.

True or false:

1. A Jewish girl is snatched by God to play a role in the drama of salvation.

2. A supreme fiction bursts into bloom around a Jewish girl impregnated by a shepherd or a soldier one starless night.

3. An angel, determined to pave the way for a rabbi he reveres, cuddles up to a Jewish girl.

4. A Jewish girl is threatened by a band of Landsmen hoping to use her to invent a messiah with a birth record and provocative ideas.

Complete this sentence: Mary is

1. an easy mark.

2. chosen at random from a crowd of Jewish women in the marketplace.

3. an adulteress.

4. a divine conduit.

5. a victim of rape by the Roman soldier, Panthera.

6. a victim of rape by one of her family or friends.

from **FARMER TROVES: March 25, In the Year of...**

March is the meatiest month

Mutable month   malleable month

Manysplendoredmoonmottledmarvel of the metaphysical

Month of messages, motherhood, margins, myth

Matchless measureless month of merger midstream

Moored month made map made mystery made magic

Multiplicitous misunderstood misdiagnosed month

Multiflorous modelmonth of the marketable

    At the waning of the moon

        Plant houseleeks
    Sow beets, borage, cabbage
    Sow violets and gillyflowers

    Plant beans, fennel and sweet marjoram
        (note: sweet marjoram likes richer soil than violets;
        too much shade will pale its green

    Graft raspberry bushes and plant in full sun

    Sow lettuce

        (it comes up quickly, grows thickly

            it is not firmly rooted

                when you want to eat it,

            pull it up root and all

Take care that your attire is neatly and simply arranged

Be a woman of valour, her worth is far above that of rubies

It is March 25, the moon wanes

THE SKY ARRIVES

THE WOVEN CHILD

I

And what if a soul
fall into a body…

And if it gaze into pure light…
And if something grow into life…

As the spider spins its web
    she spins him of herself,

AND LEAVES A MEMORY

life-bestower, nurturer,

agent of futurity

oh, woven child
    you must not unravel

she webs and warps with finest, strongest yarn

II

Listen:

Thou shalt never forget thy mother and what she has done for thee…For she
carried thee long beneath her heart as a heavy burden, and after thy months
were accomplished she bore thee.

Three long years she carried thee upon her shoulder and gave thee her breast
to thy mouth, and as thy size increased her heart never once allowed her to
say,

"Why should I do this?"

She is and remains a mother
even though her child die,

though all her children die.

For at one time she carried you under her heart.
And you do not go out of her heart ever again

ALL THIS NO MAN KNOWS

GRANDEURS AND DESOLATIONS

their eyes pierce a single distance

in which there is this news

which is

no news—

a virgin giving birth

Plato, Pythagoras, Alexander the Great
born of virgins,
and beetle come of donkey,
wasp of horse,
snake of corpse,
Laksmi of the churning sea—

as in net
as in trap

AS IN PREPARE HER FOR CONFINEMENT

why not a child without a man

from *A VARIORUM CONCERNING THE MARVELS OF WOMAN*

You must forget not the gape of her amaze

Nor remise the process of her will
… …

Yea, though the lore may calligraphy her as a wild card forsworn,
          gravid and failed of spirit

As a wild card when it is casualty…

… …

For a brief moment fate mistakes her,
          but a great compel will guide her back

A SMALL ANATOMY OF FEELING

That which installs itself in the mind embraces sound

Rebounding,
              rounding the fecund earth

Birth, as in what is not, as in one makes one,
                              is a mighty absence to understand

(and there are those who fail to get their lessons done)

Dun is the color of submission

Unfledged, she leafs through what has been nothing never
Never to be what she is/ or could /or hope to be
Bewitched by dictions (fictions) on the surface—

Face naming that which she must save, polished like an apple—

Apple of the eye, *amour* of town and street, apple of the cheek
Eaten with a dab of honey for a sweet year

Ear to *who am I* in the suddenly-arriving *what-comes-next*
Next to being, next to delivery, next to undergone
Gone parenthetical but now revived as her eye
Spies the sudden trespass of his unexpected welcome—

Succumbing, coming unto him in full sun this morning

Mourning what she need not beguile or lie beside

THE LIGHT CANNOT BE EXPLAINED

Here   now

      all things being seen   to be seen
              seen before

       gathering, crowding in—

true woman   is she that —

     or paradox—

       not simple

            a complexity

   extending her hand
            kneeling now

      inferior to the angel

        contrite   submissive

         ready to be used

          EAGER TO BE USED

  symbol and source

    virgin and mother

viewfinder, through which to gaze and find the face of God

Is this innocence interpreted

                                interrupted   intrepid

Is this virginity enslaved

                    or liberated

                          (for Ave read Eva for Eva read Eve)

                or terrified here

      knuckles whitening   sounds stiff in the throat

      (already having said nay or tried to—

              but duressed   tormented

                tortured prior to this light-blazed scene

a freedom without will

a freedom named obedience

from **ODES AND ODDMENTS**

Mary had a little lamb
His genes were white as snow
And everywhere that Mary went
The lamb was sure to know...

He followed her to bed one day
It was against the rule
He urged the virgin stay and pray
Was Mary game or tool?

One day the lamb went out to play
He said his heart stayed near
He traveled far and wide away
And so caused Mary tears

Why does the lamb love Mary so?
The ages how they've cried
Why, Mary loves the lamb you know
Apart they'll ne'er be pried

from ***THUNDER, SWEET LONGING***

> Love me loudly or in whispers,
> love me so the long, deep night
> is aware of me
> and breaks
> into day with a seamless song…

The night was deep and long, an untamed beast, a cormorant fishing for food…

Her blood budded, her mane unloosened and she galloped through the dark
like a wild horse through a speeding dream…

She was exhausted at dawn
when the blues and greens
took their places among the red moments
and the shower of gold broke
in undulating waves
through the margins of the clouds

from **ODES AND ODDMENTS**

A SONG OF MYSTERY AS MASTERY

I sing of a maiden,
A matchless maiden,
King of all kings
For her son she's taken.

He comes there so still,
His mother's yet a lass.
He's like the dew in April
That falleth on the grass.

He comes there so still
To his mother's bower.
He's like the dew in April
That falleth on the flower.

He comes there so still
To where his mother lay.
He's like the dew in April
That falleth on the spray.

Mother and maiden
Was never none but she—
Well may such a lady
God's mother be.

—Anonymous (Early English)

WHO/WHAT IS IT COMES?

Out of a vast silence, a spring spray, a drench of dew, all so still

into the cave of her body?

For mother read lover

For "like dew in April/That falleth on the flower" read

"like dew in April/That falleth to de-flower…"

String theorists concede that their equations
are approximations to an unknown theory they call M-theory

standing for matrix, magic,
mystery of mother

as in mother of all theories
as in mother of us all

Only such a one can mother the son of God

from *A DISQUISITION ON UNBEARABLE CONUNDRUMS OF BEING*

There were giants in the earth in those days, and also after that, when the sons of God came in unto the daughters of men, and they bare children to them, the same became mighty men which were of old, men of renown.
— Genesis 6:4

Gabriel, what really happened here?

> divine husband
> > bringer of seed,
> father of the god,

Lucky one, is it *you* who have been chosen

"to follow the brush," to ensnare the "fugitive sensibility,"
> *genius locus* of her place?

COME
"IN
UNTO HER."

from *A DISQUISITION ON UNBEARABLE CONUNDRUMS OF BEING*

Virgin, select from the following consummations
devoutly to be urged:

1. A stream shoots from god's mouth through a lean tube: lift your skirt

2. Your gluttonous, famished vagina bares its teeth: consume the semen

3. He has hoarded the precious flow in the dove's beak; seek it there

4. He will sow the seed in your ear; listen for it

5. A shower will wet your lips: tongue it into your mouth

and swallow

The point is lament
The point is grief
The point is melding a muddle of Marys
        Myrionymos—she of many names

      Conjured in the name of Mariamne, Semitic God-Mother
      Invoked in the name of Aphrodite-Mari
      Called by names that restore the dead:
          Juno, Blessed Virgin
          Isis, Stella Maris, Ishtar
          Queen of Heaven, Empress of Hell

      Lady of *tout le monde*

A name by any name

    Inside the name: *âme*, soul

      AND REGISTRATION

Will to be seen,
    urge to be known

      Each portrait is a name, a flag of assurance
      Guarantor of place and face

(but a sword will pass through her soul)

    Ephraem of Syria names her bride and mother of Jesus—
          son-consort, he

Ephraem dubs her   Ark   Garden of Paradise
                                        Gate of Heaven

Ceaseless multiplication to make her

                        lay of the land
                        timelessness circulating

                EN-GODDED

        I conjure her chasing stray sheep
        I invoke her gathering figs
        I call her restorer of soil, plower, tiller, dead header
        I name her pruner of olive wood, maker of fire, fanner of flame
        I come upon her wind-blown, barely sheltered under scrub oak
        I see her huddled as tax collectors pound at the door

                Give us our daily bread
                Forgive us our debts

        I know her staggered, staggering, trapped by a sudden blow,
                great winds beating still
        I name her tumbler, flailer, faller into candors too deep to reveal

                (and a sword will pass through her soul)

from **ODES AND ODDMENTS**

"You cannot own my soul," she said
He frowned, but said he would not grieve
"I know some souls are mine to grab
And yours, I see, adorns your sleeve."

"You cannot take my name," she said
"It's here and there and everywhere."
"I'll pluck and tweak," he made reply,
"And nab some mmmms *afloat in air."*

"You cannot have my heart," she said
He smiled and winked his eye,
"I do not want your heart, said he—
I do not aim so high!"

Because she is a woman— young, pleasing to the eye

Because beneath her blue robe—

>   (color of constancy
>   color of sorrow
>   color of pain—

>   (depending on light
>   depending on clouds
>   depending on the lattice of feathers—

an opening, moist and tight   pregnant with the unspoken

>   provides relief...

>   EMPOWERS MAN OR GOD

from **ODES AND ODDMENTS**

A PRIMER ON PROXIMITY

Yes, Mary birthed a wondrous boy
He was her joy, her life, God's pride
But he had vital work to do
"My future beckons nigh," he cried

So Mary turned her grieving cheek
She wailed and keened and made deep moan
Sackcloth nor ashes healed her woe
It honed its knives on sky's cold stone

Adieu, adieu, she steps aside
With mama close a son's half-grown
He needs his space; he can't gaze back
His life's a work to forge alone

Child and Mama must strive apart
His life, not death, will them divide
And death, not life, will them unite
Come soon, dear death, provide, provide

The world's an oyster, have you heard
And sons take off, the young are birds
And mothers cannot know just why
The work of being *bids them* fly

from **THE CANTO OF THE PEARL**

CHIME, CLOSED MIND

> *And as she had awakened me with her voice so she guided me with her light…*

I told you the world
Was your oyster, its surface
Rough, its outlines unkempt,
Its passion the freight
of one grain of sand.

How simply I knew.

You found it in a shallow bed
Where waters flushed warm.

Adoze, it clutched
Rose reef and shoal.

While you stood by
A sea star trapped the world
In its vise-pincer arms,
Pried open its utility,
And sucked up its plump center

You kept vigil, helpless
You were very young to walk alone.

I had taught you to be tender,
To request admission.
To honor the purpose of pearl.

Forgive me.

I dwelt inland,
Unschooled by the sea.

A DISCOURSE OF QUERY AND REPLY

And it came to pass, that after three days they found him in the temple…and his mother said unto him, Son, why hast thou thus dealt with us…I have sought thee sorrowing…And he said unto them, How is it that ye sought me? Wist ye not that I must be about my Father's business? And they understood not the saying which he spake unto them.
—Luke 2:46-50

"But, Mater
You have been the cause of anguish."

"My son, thou art grown…
cast thine eyes upon her that gave thee birth
and provided all good things for thee,
  And do not banish me from your sight,
  And do not make your voice hate me, nor your hearing.

 Do not be ignorant of me anywhere or any time."

"Moodre,
You have withheld honor."

"My son, thou art grown…
Cast thine eyes upon her that held her five-pound babe, loved
Your face, and averted her eyes from your bony limbs,
  And do not banish me from your sight,
  And do not make your voice hate me, nor your hearing."

"Moder,
You have withheld praise."

"My son, thou art grown…
Cast thine eyes upon her that knew you could do anything
But knew not how to let you know.
  And do not banish me from your sight,
  And do not make your voice hate me, nor your hearing."

"Mama,
You have taught me grievance;
I cannot float on seas we've failed to swim."

"But son, thou art grown…your unsailed seas bequeath me grief.

 Must I bare my breasts?

(they are no more)
Shall I score my face, my chest?
(my years proclaim their trace)
Though I be mute, unseen, do not be ignorant of me

Cast thine gaze upon me
forever in your heart.
And in my heart forever
you'll not drown."

from ***CODEX ATLANTICUS, FOLIO 9***

Just as a stone thrown into water becomes the center
and cause of various circles and fills the surrounding
space with infinite likenesses of itself
and appears all in all
and all in every part

—Leonardo da Vinci

from *A DISQUISITION ON UNBEARABLE CONUNDRUMS OF BEING*

SELECT TWO:

       1. Mornings like this fragments are hard to find...

       2. Mornings like this the future demands an audience lest its premise disappear...

       3. Mornings like this syllables spread anarchies in the sun...

       4. Mornings like this labor to archive subjects/objects of faith...

       5. Mornings like this agency may be braid of rope around the neck...

       6. Mornings like this the labyrinth holds invention at bay

            MORNING AND MAZE ARE ONE——

CAN SHE/WILL SHE MAKE HER WAY OUT OF THIS

The angel   have we forsaken/forgotten him?

                 Shall we blame or pity him?

Flap flap

    His wings snapflap

           and will not still

        (can angels be blamed?)

      A contagion descends

          HAIL MARY

as in shots from the prior blue
               out of the blue

        as in pellets of punctuation

         Point of departure

         Point of entry

    PERIOD   COMMA   SPACE

               PUNCTUM

                 ●

                  (can the angel be pitied?)

from *A BOOK OF RUBBINGS AND ELSEWAYS*

last night my fingers flamed in rain

they said nothing could stop them

I watched…………

        they flew

……………………………………………

      shall we wing away

into that sundrunk-moon-waxed-star-plugged-finger-filled sky

sail right into it

        space is there…………………

…………………………………………………………………………

          naysayer,
             break
          and fly

from **THE BOOK OF MANDATE AS HELOTRY**

Is it front man to gods, this urge—

Whatever it is that sizes me up
Alights and harvests
      my quick swivel

and vagrant trust
in what is uttered to butter me up—

                            oh how
his hearken creeps into me
though what I hear I fear…

No fire sears my ears
or serpents through my blood,
no nay rears
under cover of lull and numbness

Must I do what I have always done—
in a cold sweat and daring nothing,
acquiesce, grip his hand and bleed his way…

CLOAK, PERFECT CLOUD

Then what do you love, you extraordinary stranger?

Forewarning, prophecy—

darkness spread-eagles from heaven,
             between jet streams duly revved—

Organ of Showers,
        Helmet of Lust—

Thunder, perfect Inundation.
Cast forth lightning, perfect Thrust.

The Lord hath his way in the whirlwind, under cover of wind kite,
and in the aftermath *cumulo-stratus* will be dust at his feet.

O, Io, be not afraid to enter the dim forest.

Frighted she flies—

wing-fleet feet
        flee from the sudden black-blazed noon—

                              yet fails to find escape.

Knocked out,
        breathless
Beneath the many-seeded quince,

                   SHE WANTS NOTHING OF THIS

O, Io, I will O-wn you

Desire snares her in its stricken cold-mist net,
taboos the sun from shedding light on dark.

Mantled by the mid-day air,

        she is the toy of innocence;
                she fears the brunt of bliss.

He towers high and splays his draperies wide,
He invades the dim forest, aimed for her hide.

IO

Chosen, prey—owned and owed

    Rod of **I**:
                Zeus will stake his claim this day

    Round of **O**:
                the globe she's doomed long years to roam—
                white Moon-cow goaded by a looming fly—

But now is now,

Come, Zeus
      —BECAUSE YOU CAN—

Plunge, release, and soar…

NUANCE AND NAMING

Jill of all trades

~~mistress of none/~~

mistress of which one

Lady of Angels, Door of Paradise, Star of Morning, Lady of Patriarchs,
of Prophets, of Apostles, of Martyrs, of Confessors, of Virgins,
of all the Saints, of Harlots, Thieves, Usurers, Murderers,
Adulterers, every guise, disguise and shape of

Being

Mary—

If you be all these things

does the cosmos/god long for you

or you for it/him

from *A PROLEGOMENON OF BENEDICTINE LITURGY*
AS PEREGRINE SONG

Thou art the window, the door and the veil,
the courtyard and the house, the temple, the earth,

lily in thy virginity, rose by thy sufferings.

Thou art the closed garden,
the fountain of the garden that washes all who are defiled,
purifies all who are corrupted,
brings back life to the dead

…Thou art the break of day, the light that knows no darkness

Overbright

      Everbright

            INCESSANT SCOUR OF LIGHT

OH LIGHT BE NOT EXPLAINED

from *A DISCOURSE ON PROGENY AS* ERWARTUNG

BARRENS

Rabbi Yohanan: "Why were the three matriarchs barren so long?"

Answer A: "O my dove," God said,
            "why did I make you barren?
            Because I desired
            to hear your thoughts.
                            As it is written
            your voice is sweet and your face is comely."

Answer B: "I wanted you abject, obedient,
            pliable as clay,
                    soft as down."

PUTTY, pretty one

FALLOWS

A pure virgin is a fortress

She is a castle where a tower stands
        And is encircled by walls

PRISON, pussy cat

CHROMA AND VICISSITUDE

The angel is an idea

The idea is an analogy

The analogy is a commonplace

The commonplace is an arrangement

The arrangement is a residue

>angel, maiden
>pillars, loggias, walled terraces
>ruins and jagged rocks
>skeins of cloud
>a door ajar
>lily
>leaves in an urn

>arcades opening onto a distant garden

The garden was/ is an idea

>[the] *gate shall remain shut*
>
>*it shall not be opened*
>
>*and no one shall enter by it*

from **A TREATISE ON PAINTING**

...some days ago I saw the picture of an Angel who, in making the Annunciation, seemed to be trying to chase Mary out of her room with movements showing the sort of attack one might make on some hated enemy; and Mary, as if desperate, seemed to be trying to throw herself out of the window. Do not fall into errors like these.

— Leonardo da Vinci

It is time to speak of the lies
        of images, omissions, insertions—

    imitations of reality,

            but whose reality, Leonardo?

    For you she's in nature—

            you've lavished so much attention
                        on rock formations along your raised horizon
            varieties of grass in the lawn
            cloud convocations

            and the shadow the archangel casts
        obliterating most of what's imagined growing there

            and she, lovely, composed—"great grace of shadows and of lights is added
to the faces of those who sit" beside the darkness of brown plasterwork—her right arm
almost deformed, too far forward,

            reaching out at an impossible angle—

                    FOR WHAT

—Botticelli, Campin, van Eyck—for you

she's indoors all decked out in luscious silk and satin,
surrounded by finery—tied-back drapery, carved benches,
a rug or tiled floor, loggias
and archways beyond her wildest ken
windows revealing *hortus conclusi* and winding paths
        slogging toward the sea

And what of all those blues and golds, so rife with wealth

    in her life there's only red from madder juice
    and yellow from kaolin clay
       and a linen shift all frayed

The truth also is a small opening high up on the wall
A floor that's hard-packed dirt
And beyond the room, villagers working the fields,
donkeys dragging threshing boards over newly harvested wheat

AND EVERYWHERE, INSIDE AND OUT, *WORLD-MOTHERING* DUST

    For all of you
this is an event reduced to a book she cannot read
a lily she does not smell
a lectern she never owned

She might as well comb her hair with a stiletto heel
Make of her body a cloud of white tulle
Carry a watering can and wear shapely wooden clogs
Fake glamour in a black bare-back gown
Crouch on the ground flipping coins
Pop a pogo stick between her legs and levitate

    SHE COULD BE ANYONE   ANYWHERE   ANYTIME

She could be sitting in her slip, bored,
bored to death, the intercom
image appearing out of nowhere,
announcing a stranger

    (*prima materia*, take a deep breath

    (for divinity to enter the world,
       your mystery must be experienced

Her eyes will go wide, not expecting this

Her ears have encountered only silence

    and the soft moan of a dove
    (OOOOOOOOOOOOOO

The trees thin
The cumulus sky crackles ever so quietly
Somewhere a rainbow breaks

      too loud now
         too strident

      He's gotten in

Hail comes in pellets
    (heavy hitters

     She will be patient
     and hear him out
        though what she really wants is to get back under the covers
        that are damask, but a lie—
          (rough-hewn flax is what she'd have)

Or she could be blending a batch of myrrh
and roses to deodorize the foul
stench of the room that opens out
not on a vista of budding poplars
but on sewage,
piles of it
come to rot at the side of the road
just there, in front of her door
     where broken planks of wood lean
     and bleating sheep wait to be herded up the hill

But here's this guy breezing in

        (Titian, El Greco paint his feet unplanted on the ground
          (is he preparing for a quick getaway
             or must he be higher on the picture plane
        (Tintoretto catches him in mid-flight, a show-off, he
        (Martini and Crivelli force him to his knees

The breeze may be the whisper of something
     she is in danger of losing

     (the breeze may be her destiny

or his feathers could begin to moult
        (transaction of feathers,
        (light as a feather
           in the face of all that dust she can't escape

or she could cringe at wings,
                    voracious, unfurled,
trying to scoop her up, knock her down,
drown her in their soft pile,

snuff out any NO she stashes in her mind,
or the wind could whip his feathers
and blow the townsfolk quickly to her side

        (Today, she knows no one will arrive in time...)

        Certainly not those people tending their gardens,
            (as if anyone had topiary trees
                as Rogier van der Weyden (possibly Memling) shows

                    (read fields of barley and wheat
                        and plows, plenty of plows

In his eyes, pools of light map no pollution, only flame
In hers, no flecks, no threads mar the cobalt calm

            until his hail scumbles their surface

        What is she to make of it

Her lids lower

Chrysalises, her eyes close on their private dusk
            (she's already seen her share of Roman crucifixions

        (perhaps the future is there and her eyes seek the great above
                where son and mother will be united
        (perhaps she conjugates the months—
                (nine is real—
                (a number done on her

        (perhaps she dabbles with using rue to end the thing

                SHE'S GOT A CHOICE AFTER ALL

For the child she will have boundless love

For posterity the memory of being

For her life no proper translation

from ***MEANINGS AND MENTORS***

I cannot fix my object;
'tis always tottering and reeling by a natural giddiness:
I take it as it is at the instant I consider it;
I do not paint its being.
*   I paint its passage…*

—Michel de Montaigne, "Of Repentence"

Comes now the presto of his offensive

Name the eye, the foot, the outstretched hand

    ("our minds are dark when things are close, are here")

The scene unfurls in which he'll catch the longing of the girl

    (Things slip away from the intentions that have located them

                      (but not today

                              not this day)

Frisson of fear or desire…

    lust or restraint…

Thou art favored…

        I am favored…

She is favored…

    And with her YES a future world takes shape

Woman
                Alone of all her sex

                              (On a ladder
                        (rising up or climbing down)

                              (On a brush
                      (being written or suddenly erased)

                            shaped and

        TOLD BY MEN

      (narrative/language is a re-vision)

And she
        nothing knowing,
                nor ever letter reading

Holds her tongue

For if she says nay they will rub her with oil and roast her on coals,
Plunge her seaward with a stone around her neck,
Lop off her breasts and slice her tongue...

             So, for her nay a future bates its breath

And if she say yea, even in Arcady death resides...

from *A BOOK OF RUBBINGS AND ELSEWAYS*

OF UBIQUITOUS WILL

And this he said: Hail, thou art exalted … [Hail] thou art adored …
… Bequeathed [betrothed] ……… soul in heaven, bone on earth

And this he said: ……… between your limbs …… Tender of Gardens, Mother ….
…… a son will be ……… who is the sun ……

And this he said: through your loins all becoming will come … …
Harmonies of blood ……… durations of eternity…

And this he said: … each year spelt yellows then greens anew ……
Thou art chosen ……… green greener than the great inundation

And this he said: [as] ….. Ka seethes into thee … open your mouth
Warm your mortar for the pestle of this seed

And so for me was he desirous
And so he spoke but was denied

For this I, Hekenus, said: I've not finished braiding my hair, kohling my eyes
……… I've just cut the curled sidelock from my brow

For this I, Hekenus, said: dates I've picked await … [their eating] …………......
… I ……… advent and abandonment ……

For this I, Hekenus, said: meantime meanwhile… [as all] existing
……… to bake [bread], to spin, to weave, to carve my name

For this I, Hekenus, said: I've yet … [becoming] ……… let me become
Not precedent or augury …… me ……… aftermath in afterglow

For this I, Hekenus, said: summer hours are long … myrrh [perfumes] …
…… wild geese soar in a craze of flight

For this I, Hekenus, said: fields are rampant with corn, with sugar cane and cotton,
I will be grinding girl, driver of chariots, priestess, hairdresser, supervisor of the cloth

For this I, Hekenus, said: I will be treasurer, steward, composer, mourner, musician
weaver, dancer, designer of wigs, choreographer of pleasures for the king

For this I, Hekenus, said: I will not enter the plot of your desire to make me legible to
the ages nor ……… wear a false beard or male garb to steal away

For this I, Hekenus, said: before *Khamsin* drives dust ………
……….. parched soil cracks again … ……

For this I, Hekenus, said: ….. useless to seek…. lamentations save [no] ……
[I] follow my heart and its happiness, seize day and night, the very air burning

For this I, Hekenus, said: I will wear woven garlands around my throat,
Pin lotus to my hair, bathe Nileside ………… stones of the great light

For this I, Hekenus, said: your mysteries are not welcome
My mysteries I wield but will not yield

And so to me, tender of gardens, made he tender
And so by me was he denied

from ***MARKS, MYSTERIES, AND MELODIES***

DIPTYCH

     I

     And, behold, thou shalt conceive in thy womb, and bring forth a son,
     and shalt call his name JESUS. —Luke 1: 31

What will you do, bugle, if I refuse?

     I am your pitch-pipe
                   (when I am mute?)

     I am your droit
                   (when I am fugitive?)

I, your gasconade, your crap-shoot.

Without me what alibi, what hornblow?
Without me what howdy do if no
intrauterine write-in awaits your baton?

I, sang-froid that eludes your foray.

I, exposer of your simulacrum.

Your counterglow rebuffed
        as it *aubades* this *divertissement*
largo after hub bub,
glissando after bray—

        brasswork come to nothing,
               a herald in the cold.

What will you do, bugle?

To whom,
     to what,
          shall I pray?

II

And Mary said, Behold the handmaid of the Lord;
be it unto me according to thy word. —Luke 1:38

What will you do, desire, when I comply?

      I am your dulcimer
                        (when I am drum?)

      I am your fealty
                        (when I am tweedledee cum dum?)

I, your perch, your percolator.

Without me what likelihood, what gadfly
gadabout? Without me what thing
with feathers in the soul?

I, thunderbolt that mums your song and dance.

I, betrayer of your pitch and toss.

High flyers and fancy flights I've spurned
              will hunt for me in vain
                    to surf the tides and network with the stars.

What will you do, desire?

To whom,
      to what
                    (and where)

           shall I atone?

The real, the true song
      shapes cues of seduction and might

We are water

                  we are wager

      we will be outlived by our intentions

     her destiny:
            to signify something

     her damnation:
            to signify nothing

HER CONDITION: *WOMANHOOD*

his: a collage of thirsts
          slaked by lust

Beware, Mary,
      hungers are irreconcilable with dreams

Then the womb of Mary,
        like the fleece of Gideon, was drenched with dew

And the rod of Gabriel, like the rod of Aaron,
        brought forth buds, and bloomed blossoms

                Mary
                        like a snake, the rod writhes

Come Gabriel, blow your horn,
     the cow's in the meadow,

         the maid's oh so torn—

Angel be bird,
     shadow you make
         be bird again

     Quid enim futurum fuit si—what would have happened if…

         what truly happened here…

hover, dove while we figure this out

from **MEANINGS AND MENTORS**

VERUM FACTUM: *what is true is what we have made true*

—Giambattista Vico, *De Italorum Sapientia*

from **_ODES AND ODDMENTS_**

Will you come with me, sweet maid
Through the de rigueurs *of pose,*
Of nimbus, and veiled waylay
       (The patron low-balls the exposé
       (The superhero foretells the foreclose
Where heaven steers continuous
Where none obtrude and none oppress.
Sweet maiden, come without duress.

       Round and round the buck will go
       Just what is sought we may not know

There's nothing like the present, maid,
The past is gone, the future shade.
So come with me, and come we will
On fields of foam and sheets of silk.
Sweet maiden, I will be your eyes
I ask you only spread your thighs.

       Round and round the buck will go
       Why now, why here we will not know

And so the god lays claim his prey
(How can she dodge the ricochet
Of shower of gold and silver tongue?
The god gives not a hoot she's young
And thrown a loop by his foreplay.
The god will make his move today…
And there's not the teeniest way to see,
Sweet maiden, that his joy is thee.

       Round and round the buck will go
       And where it stops we cannot know

BREATH AND BEWILDERMENT

I

DISQUIET

Anguish of the not yet

      (Not of wonder   (not of lust   (not of need

Stagger of the yet to be

      (hard blow of worry   (generalized fret

            (some of our daughters have been ravished—(Nehemiah)

                   genes do not/will not blend

               (this I will know centuries later

Safety retreats
Revoked
By a rush of angels caressing my thighs

      seeds of unease leaf in a deep cave of fleeing

What manner of mind, of speech
What fear ignites this history

(A disquiet in my ear leaps

II

REFLECTION

Fear not when the light of creation drops
And takes blaze in you
Reflect and reflect as your son shall be a reflection
and he will be undersized at the start
and he will grow and grow into an icon of boy,
a paradigm of man, divine,
an axefall of distinction and separation

III

INQUIRY

Born of an original text

Only begotten son…

> *not my son*

> > *(he cannot say it, hence he'll turn away*

Must I die of him?

Year after year in the son's face
A sunface eclipsed

> (To exist is to be perceived…

Year after year in my mined eye
His mind's eye

> (when all external perception fails, there is this…

his face is never/
> must never/
> > will never

> > > be empty or erased

> so, too, his soul…

IV

SUBMISSION

Her knees hit the ground

And her eyes…

> windows of the soul…

(The white of her eye is not widely extended,
> therefore she is not shameless;

nor is it concealed,

therefore we can rely on her.

Handmaid—slaveservant
Rise to this occasion

Because I am woman teeming with life, because
I have choice, because I am
virgin in love with being virgin—
unpossessed and unpossessable

by any man

because that which resembles only itself has no reality

V

MERIT

Alone, unaligned
   Neither now nor ever simply SELF

   ANGELS, BOW OUT

from **MEANINGS AND MENTORS**

: *Let no one call Mary the Mother of God, for Mary was but a woman,*
and it is impossible that God should be born of a woman.

— Pope Anastasius I

THE WANTON SUBLIME

Cut to Mary's face
Cut to troubled reeds
        Oh my heart is woe, Mary she said so, for
                to see my dear son go, and sons I have no more.
Cut to the winding road
Cut to sunrise
Cut to Mary's torso
        Oh my heart is woe …
Cut to her finger crooked in his direction
Cut to her thighs
        Oh my son, my son who will forsake me.
Cut to her hands on her mons
Cut to her hands on her abdomen
        Oh my son, my son must you forsake me?
Cut to winds lowing, hips writhing
Cut to her eyes fixed on definition
Cut to the sky attempting arrival
        Oh my son, my son why have you forsaken me?
Cut to fear and wonder and wavering light
Cut to radiance reeking of why
Cut to the gulf between earth and radiance
        Oh my heart is woe …
Cut to brittle waves and turbulent seas
        of fugitive, turnsole blue
Cut to the magic of disappearance
        and the trembling that knows no clemency
Cut and cut and cut again…

Knowing she does not/cannot know
Knowing she is isolate and *sfumato*
        Oh my son, my son why have you forsaken me?

Cut to her soul which is body
        which is the dust
                of an inescapable need

Cut to the garden of her soul which is landmined

Cut to survival

        as possibility
                as mark…

FOR THOSE WHO ARE TO COME

That I have been…

That I have…

To remind…

My life…

LIGHT BE NOT EXPLAINED